TEACHING CHILDREN ABOUT BACKYARD BIRDS

Catherine Lazaroff

Photo Credits:

Ron Austing: p. 12B; 15 (Eastern Towhee); 24; 26; 29 (Tufted Titmouse); 31; 42; 52; 53 (Eastern Bluebird); 54; 58
Jeff Fishbein: p. 25; 56
Marvin Hyett: p. 11 all
Kaytee Products: p. 31; 61
Larry Kimball: p. 3 (Wood Duck); 9 (Rufous Hummingbird)
Peter LaTourette: p. 23 (Vermilion Flycatcher); 35 (Cedar Waxwing); 39; 59 (Lazuli Bunting)
Rafi Reyes: p. 10B; 16; 18T; 30; 34; 40; 41; 49; 57
Rob & Ann Simpson: p. 1 (Rose-breasted Grosbeak); 4 (House Finch); 13; 19; 20; 22; 28; 32; 43 (Red-breasted Nuthatch); 45; 47
John Tyson: p. 4; 6; 7; 8; 10T; 12T; 14; 18B; 36; 37T; 44; 46; 51; 55
Maleta M. Walls: p. 50 (Carolina Chickadee)

Dedication

To David and Cherie Lazaroff, for teaching their daugther to love birds, herps, and binkies

© T.F.H. Publications, Inc.

KT 104

Distributed in the UNITED STATES to the Pet Trade by T.F.H. Publications, Inc., 1 TFH Plaza, Neptune City, NJ 07753; on the Internet at www.tfh.com; in CANADA by Rolf C. Hagen Inc., 3225 Sartelon St., Montreal, Quebec H4R 1E8; Pet Trade by H & L Pet Supplies Inc., 27 Kingston Crescent, Kitchener, Ontario N2B 2T6; in ENGLAND by T.F.H. Publications, PO Box 74, Havant PO9 5TT; in AUSTRALIA AND THE SOUTH PACIFIC by T.F.H. (Australia), Pty. Ltd., Box 149, Brookvale 2100 N.S.W., Australia; in NEW ZEALAND by Brooklands Aquarium Ltd., 5 McGiven Drive, New Plymouth, RD1 New Zealand; in SOUTH AFRICA by Rolf C. Hagen S.A. (PTY.) LTD., P.O. Box 201199, Durban North 4016, South Africa; in JAPAN by T.F.H. Publications. Published by T.F.H. Publications, Inc.

Manufactured in the
United States of America
by T.F.H. Publications, Inc.

Contents

Age should not be a barrier to starting a child in the enjoyable hobby of birdwatching.

WHY TEACH CHILDREN ABOUT BIRDS?

Birds are one of the easiest forms of wildlife to watch. They can be seen almost anywhere, at any time. Some birds have adapted well to urban and suburban living, and many can be found right in your own backyard. Because birds are so easy to find, birdwatching is a great way to introduce your children to the natural world around them.

By watching birds, your children will develop concentration and find reasons to spend more time outdoors. Bird identification skills teach children to pay attention to detail. Studying bird books is a fun way to hone reading skills, and birdwatching videos are a great substitute for cartoons.

Learning about birds can also broaden a child's horizons, leading to questions and lessons about other habitats, even other countries. Birds know no national boundaries; many migrate thousands of miles each year. The more your child learns about birds, the more he or she will think about the other places that birds visit and how things that happen in faraway places can affect the birds that visit the United States.

An appreciation for birds as wild creatures can teach a child to respect the lives of all wild animals. Birds are remarkably resilient, despite their sometimes fragile appearance. Watching birds fend off rivals, cope with changes in the weather, and sing brightly in the morning sun will help children look on all living things as having full and interesting lives.

As children grow, so do the possibilities for birdwatching activities and the benefits that children and families can enjoy from birdwatching. This book has its foundation in your own backyard. Your child can see many birds from your own windows, and even more in your garden. But don't limit yourself to your yard. Birds don't recognize property lines, and learning about them can be a great excuse to extend your child's boundaries to include your neighborhood, your town, and your state. This book will help you guide your children in activities and outings that will help them learn about birds and their world—your world.

Learning about birds is part of what any child should know about nature, broadening horizons and aiding an early understanding of ecology.

Basic birding is simple to learn, requires little equipment, and can be lots of fun at any age.

A Song Sparrow, one of many small brown birds that children may find challenging to identify.

Chapter One

WHAT IS A BIRD?

What do you think of when you think of a bird? Most people think of a singing robin, a soaring hawk, or migrating geese. But not all birds sing, and not all birds fly. Some birds, like penguins, have wings that are too small for flight but work well for swimming. One type of bird, the kiwis from New Zealand, has almost no wings at all.

To start teaching your child about birds, it may help to know what makes a bird unique. There are a few things that all birds have in common. All birds are warm-blooded, have two legs, and lay eggs. But only one thing separates a bird from all other animals—its feathers.

A Blue Jay feather.

Feathers are made of keratin, the same material in human hair and fingernails. Most birds have two main kinds of feathers—down and contour. Down feathers are usually found near the bird's body and are the type used in feather pillows. They are soft and fluffy, and they help keep the bird warm. Many birds use their own down feathers to line their nests, keeping their eggs secure and warm.

Contour feathers, those found on the outer layers, give a bird its color and sleek appearance. They camouflage some birds so they cannot be seen by predators. Other birds have bright colors to help them attract mates. Contour feathers are held together by tiny hooks that fasten onto each other like Velcro or a zipper. They overlap to keep out wind and rain. When a bird preens its feathers, it reattaches the hooks in the right places so the feathers lie just right. Contour feathers also enable most birds to fly.

Birds have another adaptation that allows them to fly. Most have hollow bones, so their skeletons are very light. A bird as big as your child would only weigh about half as much as he or she does, because of its lighter bones.

Telling Birds Apart

Although there are a few things that make all birds alike, in many other ways birds vary widely. Birds come in an astonishing range of sizes and shapes, from the tiny hummingbird to the enormous ostrich. They live in almost every habitat on the planet, from jungle to desert to ocean.

The Great Egret is a common but truly "different-looking" type of bird.

Some eat seeds, others eat insects, and some even eat other birds. With all these variations, how can you teach your child to tell birds apart? First, birds can be placed in general categories by where they live and what they eat. Learning some of these categories will make it easy for your child to look at a bird and yell out "It's a duck!" or "It's a hawk!" Figuring out which kind of duck or hawk comes later.

BEAKS AND BILLS

A bird's bill can tell you what food it eats, and that can tell you (generally) what kind of bird it is. Birds do not have teeth, so they use their bills to catch and hold their food. Bills are also used for straightening and cleaning feathers and for building nests.

SEED EATERS: have strong, thick bills for cracking open seeds. Sparrows, finches, and cardinals are good examples of some common seedeaters that may visit backyard feeders.

INSECT EATERS: have longer, lighter bills. Swallows and warblers are common insect eaters.

An Eastern Towhee, a typical seedeater.

BOTTOM FEEDERS: such as ducks, have broad, flat bills for scooping up plants and water insects. Most ducks and all geese fit this description.

FISH EATERS: have long, sometimes serrated bills for grasping slippery fish. Herons, terns, kingfishers, and some diving ducks are fish eaters.

SHOREBIRDS: have long, very slender bills for probing the sand for little crabs and snails to eat. Sandpipers are the quintessential shorebirds.

MEAT EATERS: have strong, hooked bills for tearing meat. Hawks, falcons, and owls all have hooked bills for eating mice and other small creatures.

NECTAR SIPPERS: have extremely long bills for slipping into flowers to find the sweet liquid inside. Hummingbirds drink nectar, as do some orioles.

The flat beak of a duck or goose is easy to recognize and helps define the group for any child.

FOLLOW THE FOOTSTEPS

The grasping talons of a Barred Owl, typical of a bird of prey.

Feet help tell you where a bird lives and what it eats. Looking at bird footprints can tell you what kinds of birds have visited your backyard.

Perching birds, the largest groups of birds, are also known as passerines. Most common backyard birds fit into this category. Most perching birds have three forward facing toes and one rear-facing toe. When the bird rests on a branch, its toes automatically lock onto the branch so that it doesn't fall off—even when it sleeps.

Waterbirds have webbed feet for swimming and for braking when they land on water. Ducks, geese, and gulls all have webbed feet.

Wading birds, such as herons, have long legs and very long toes. These help keep the birds from sinking into mud and sand when walking in shallow water.

Birds of prey, or meat-eating birds, have sharp, curved talons for catching and gripping their food. Many of these birds have trouble walking because their talons get in the way.

BIRDS OF A FEATHER FLOCK TOGETHER

Some groups of birds are best distinguished by their behavior. Woodpeckers, for example, can be easily distinguished by the way they use their strong bills to drill holes in trees. They catch insects living inside trees and under bark by drilling right through their homes. Sometimes they'll even try to drill into the wood of *your* house.

The X-shaped feet of a Red-bellied Woodpecker help it climb vertically up trees.

Flycatchers and gnatcatchers make quick flights from a perch in a tree or bush to catch insects on the wing. These short, quick flights are often the only way to catch sight of these tiny birds.

You and your children will learn to distinguish other groups of birds by behavior just by watching them. By taking time to observe the birds at your backyard feeder or birdbath, you'll quickly see differences in behavior even between similar birds like sparrows and finches.

Woodpeckers, such as the Red-headed Woodpecker, are birds that display many adaptations to digging food out of trees.

Keeping the birdbath filled is a simple chore for a child.

Chapter Two

GETTING STARTED

The only two requirements children really need to watch birds are their eyes and ears. Teaching your children to tune into the natural world around them is the first and most important step toward teaching them about birds. Try taking a walk with your child in your own backyard and talking to each other about the birds, insects, and plants you see. Listen to the sounds of birds as they fly overhead or move about in the trees or visit your birdfeeders. Once you've pointed out birds to your children, they are likely to start pointing out birds to you wherever you go.

If your child is interested in finding more birds and learning more about them, there are some pieces of basic equipment that will be helpful—even in your own backyard.

Binoculars

Binoculars magnify your view, making it easier to see specific features of a bird's plumage and to watch bird behavior "up close" without disturbing the birds. Binoculars are almost indispensable for serious birdwatching. They will expand your child's viewing world while at the same time bringing the birds closer to your child.

All binoculars have two tubes containing magnifying lenses. Most can be focused to look at things that are far away or relatively close. Some binoculars will let you focus one eyepiece differently than the other, which can be important if your child wears glasses or contact lenses.

Binoculars don't need to be expensive to be good. They vary widely in size and quality. You can get by with very simple, inexpensive binoculars, or you may choose to buy a more expensive pair that better fits your needs. Weight and ease of focus are important considerations—your child won't use binoculars that are too heavy or too hard to see through.

There are two numbers associated with every pair of binoculars—the magnification and the diameter of the front lens. The magnification tells you how many times closer an object will appear through the lenses. The larger the front lens diameter, the more light comes through the binoculars. This is important for birdwatching in low-light conditions, like on cloudy days, in dark woods, or at dusk. But larger front lenses mean more glass and, therefore, more weight.

Binoculars come in many sizes and price ranges. Be sure a child's binoculars fit the face correctly and are not too heavy.

The two barrels of binoculars can be moved farther apart or closer together. Make sure the binoculars your child will use fit your child's eyes—can you push the two barrels close enough together that your child sees a single image through them, instead of two separate images?

Many birdwatchers use 7x35 binoculars, which magnify seven times. These binoculars aren't too heavy and generally allow you to focus on birds that are fairly close to you. Binoculars with higher magnification bring birds in closer, but they have a smaller field of view. That means the area you see through the lenses is smaller, which can make it harder to find a bird, particularly if you are just learning to use binoculars.

If your child wears glasses, look for binoculars that have soft, foldable rubber eye cups. By folding back the cups, you bring your child's eyes closer to the lenses and make it easier to see through the binoculars. Attach a wide, comfortable neck strap to the binoculars that won't chafe your child's neck. Adjust the length of the strap so the binoculars rest securely against your child's chest or stomach.

A visit to a camera store or a store that sells optics will allow you and your child to try different binoculars and find a pair that fits.

USING BINOCULARS

Before your child tries to focus binoculars on a moving bird, you'll want to be sure that he or she is comfortable using binoculars. There is nothing more frustrating than catching a glimpse of an intriguing bird and being unable to focus on it with binoculars because you haven't prepared and practiced ahead of time.

With most binoculars, you focus both eyepieces at the same time using a knob or ring in the center of the two barrels. In addition, some binoculars allow you to adjust the focus of one eyepiece (usually the right one) to compensate for individual eye strengths. If your child does not have 20/20 vision, you may need to adjust separately for each eye.

Practice focusing on things that don't move. A street sign or other lettered sign is a great object to practice on, because your child will easily be able to tell you whether the letters are in focus or not. First, with your child standing next to you, focus the binoculars on the sign yourself. You should end up with a single, clear image of the letters.

Now, hand the binoculars to your child. Without adjusting the focus, push the barrels together so they are the right width for your child's eyes. Have your child look at the same sign. Can your child see the sign clearly? Have her close one eye and look through the binoculars with the other—is the image still clear? Then check the other eye.

EASY FOCUSING

The most common problem children have in using binoculars is simply finding the birds through the eyepieces. Children will often take their eyes off the bird to look at their binoculars as they bring them up to their eyes, losing the bird in the process. Here's a technique that should help your child overcome this problem.

1. Have her look at the bird without binoculars first, moving her whole head to face the bird, not just her eyes.

2. Without taking her eyes off the bird, have her raise the binoculars to her eyes and look through them.

3. Without moving her head, have your child use the focus ring to bring the birds into focus.

Using this technique keeps your child's head and eyes pointed toward the bird, so that when the binoculars come up to the eyes, they will also be pointed at the bird. Besides avoiding frustration, this can also prevent your child from accidentally looking at the sun through the binoculars, which can damage her eyes.

Start by practicing with large, slow-moving birds like ducks in a lake. Focusing on birds at a bird feeder or birdbath is another easy way to learn to find and follow birds with binoculars.

Spotting scopes on tripods allow greatly magnified, long-term looks at birds.

If one eye is clearer than the other, adjust the focus until the left eye can see clearly. Then adjust the individual focus on the right eyepiece until it is as clear as the left one. You may want to tape the right eyepiece adjustment in place so that you don't have to go through this process each time your child uses the binoculars.

CARING FOR BINOCULARS

When your child isn't using the binoculars, store them with the eyecups facing up. Cover the lenses at both ends with the protective plastic caps that came with the binoculars, and store them in their carrying case. Keep the lenses clean by blowing away dust or dirt instead of wiping it away, then using a soft cotton cloth to wipe off fingerprints. For more thorough cleaning, you can buy special lens tissue and cleaner from the store where you purchased your binoculars. Keep the binoculars in a cool, dry place. Don't store them in your car, because changing temperatures and vibrations can change the internal alignment of the lenses.

Bird Identification Guides

In the early days of birdwatching, there were no books to help naturalists identify birds in the field. These days, there are many guides to choose from. Unless you're planning a trip out of the country, the guides to shop for fall into a few basic categories: picture books, regional guides, North American guides, and specialized guides for particular groups of birds.

With the exception of picture books for young children, most bird guides are organized taxonomically by bird categories based on closely related species. They help birdwatchers narrow down the type of bird they are looking at and guide you to look at the characteristics,

Some birds, such as the Canada Goose, are found across the country; others may occur only in part of one state.

Of the many species of warblers, the Yellow Warbler is one of the most distinctive and easy to study. Children may find this group of birds difficult—even many adult birders have trouble with warblers.

The bright blue colors of a male Indigo Bunting contrast greatly with the dull brownish grays of the female.

or field marks, that spell the difference between similar birds. Visit a bookstore or library and choose a guide that is right for your child's reading level and your geographic area.

PICTURE BOOKS: For beginning birdwatchers, particularly very young enthusiasts, books with large, clear pictures that will catch a young child's interest are your best bet. Find a guide limited to birds the child is likely to find easily in your backyard or nearby parks. There are a number of guides that focus on backyard birds. Most of these guides give some basic bird information aimed at young readers.

REGIONAL GUIDES: These are guides that focus on specific areas of the country. By only including the birds that are likely to be seen in your area, these guides make it easier to narrow down the likely suspects when you and your child are trying to identify a new bird. Older children may enjoy regional guides that offer more detailed information on bird behavior, habitat, and natural history.

NORTH AMERICAN GUIDES: As your child grows older and your family plans trips to other areas, you will want to invest in a guide that covers all of North America. There are several excellent North American guides made for easy use in the field. Some use drawings to illustrate bird plumage; others use actual bird photographs. Either will aid your child in identifying unfamiliar birds.

SPECIALIZED GUIDES: For more advanced birdwatchers, there are specialized guides that focus on groups of birds that are difficult to tell apart. If your child develops a strong interest in birds, he or she may want the extra challenge of identifying difficult birds like gulls, shorebirds, or hawks. Many of these guides are made more for studying at home than carrying into the field.

Field Notebook

In Europe, many birdwatchers don't even carry field guides into the field. Instead, they take a lot of notes and draw detailed pictures of birds they are seeing for the first time, so that they can identify them later at home. Although you don't have to go to this extreme, carrying pencil and paper and encouraging your child to use them will give your child a more complete birdwatching experience.

Drawing pictures and taking notes on birds seen will cause your child to focus on individual birds and their behavior. This will help your child view birds as part of the natural world, rather than animated versions of the pictures in a field guide.

FARTHER AFIELD

Consider these other items when heading out into the field:

FIELD CLOTHING: Dress for the weather and the environment you plan to visit. If it's going to be hot, wear loose-fitting, light-colored clothing. Long pants will help avoid scratches if you're walking through brush or tall grass. In winter, bundle up and make sure your child has very good gloves—hands that are holding binoculars can't stay tucked away in warm pockets. Good shoes are important in any weather. Because many great birdwatching spots are near water, waterproof boots can be very useful.

BUG SPRAY: If you're going into a field or the woods, it's important to protect your child against bugs such as mosquitoes, ticks, and chiggers. Long-sleeved shirts and long pants provide good barriers, but sometimes additional protection is needed. Bug repellent sprays can not only prevent irritating, itchy bites that might deter your child from future outings— they can also keep your child healthy. Used judiciously, sprays containing at least 30 percent DEET can help prevent bites from ticks carrying diseases like Lyme disease. If you're concerned about spraying a young child's skin directly, spray their clothing. Tucking pant legs into socks and spraying the socks thoroughly can prevent ticks from getting to your child's skin.

SUNSCREEN: Protecting against sunburn is crucial for young children. Use a sunscreen made for children, even on cloudy days. Sunglasses that block ultraviolet light and a hat that shades the eyes will protect young faces from sunburn and let your child spend many happy hours looking through binoculars.

FOOD AND WATER: Be sure to carry food and plenty of water—for yourselves, not the birds! Even on short walks, children can get hungry and thirsty. To avoid having a rumbling tummy cut your bird walk short, carry a couple of snacks.

Its gigantic bill and distinctive colors make the Evening Grosbeak one of the easiest birds to recognize.

Chapter Three

BIRD IDENTIFICATION MADE EASY

It's easy to become frustrated when trying to identify birds. The important thing to remember is that even expert birdwatchers will be unable to identify some of the birds they spot. Here are some easy tips to help you and your child identify more of the birds you see and increase your enjoyment and knowledge of the world of birds.

Watch First, Identify Later

When you first see a bird, spend as much time looking at it as you can. Sometimes a bird will wait around while you look it up in a guidebook. More often, the bird will fly away before you finish figuring out *where* to look in the guidebook. Spend your time looking at as many details of the bird's appearance and behavior as possible. Go to the field guide only after you have seen as much of the bird as you want to see—or are able to see.

Memorize Several Important Features

Most birds resemble at least one or two other birds. Don't count on picking the one feature that will separate the bird from all similar birds. Try to always note the color and shape of as many of these features as possible:

Bill: Does it look short or long in relation to the head? Is it thick or thin?

Head: Is the head more than one color? If there are stripes on the head, where are they and what color are they? Is there a crest (a prominent tuft of feathers sticking up on the back of the head)? What color are the eyes?

Wings: Are they a different color than the bird's body? Are there stripes or bars on the wings?

Tail: Is it a different color than the bird's body? Are there any stripes or bands on the tail? Does it look long or short in relation to the rest of the body?

If you teach your child to concentrate on specific characteristics of specific features, he or she will have better luck remembering enough about a bird to then find it in a guidebook and identify it.

Field marks of the male Blue-gray Gnatcatcher include the white ring around the eye and the black tail with narrow white edges. Other features, such as the black stripe above the eye, may help determine the sex.

There are many common black birds, but east of California only the Red-winged Blackbird has bright red shoulder patches with a pale bar beneath.

Comparing size, posture, head shape, length of tail, and other features of a mystery bird with the American Robin (or another very familiar species) often helps identification.

Techniques for Remembering Features

At first, this can be pretty hard. You and your child may find yourselves frantically trying to memorize the pattern on a bird's head, only to find when you look in the guidebook that none (or all!) of the birds look like what's in your memory. But take heart—it gets easier with practice. Here are some tips to help:

1. Always try to look at the bird's features in order from head to tail—beak, head, wings, tail—remembering to take a quick overview of the body on the way.
2. Compare the bird to other, more familiar birds. Is it smaller than a duck? Bigger than a robin? Does the bird's bill look like a Blue Jay's bill, or is it more like a sparrow's?
3. Encourage your child to study the guidebook to learn some basic bill shapes and body postures. That way, your child can look at a new bird and know quickly that it has a "seed-eating bill" or clings to a tree like a woodpecker.

Using a Guidebook

Bird guides are organized into general groups of birds, like sparrows, woodpeckers, and hawks. Learning the major distinguishing features of each bird group will make it easier for your child to narrow down bird choices in the field and quickly move to the right section of the guide. There are commercially produced quick reference sheets available for many bird guides that you paste into the front or back of the book. These quick references will make it much easier to move directly to the right section to find a new bird.

Though the guidebook should always be your last resort in the field, it can be a great learning tool at other times. Encourage your child to spend time with the book at home or in the car.

Keeping a Bird List

There are conflicting opinions about keeping a bird list, which is a list of birds you have seen as well as additional information about where and when you saw a bird, along with any notable weather conditions or behavior. Some birders get so interested in listing all the birds they see, they forget to really look at the birds themselves, but, particularly for beginning birdwatchers, lists can help keep young minds interested. Lists provide a ready-made set of goals and a way to track achievements. They jog the memory, reminding your child what he or she has already seen or wants to see. Later on, they'll help bring back great memories of the first time your child saw a Pileated Woodpecker, or a roadrunner, or some other spectacular bird.

You can get bird checklists that are specific to your area by contacting a local bird club or by visiting a nearby bird sanctuary. Some web sites will allow you to download bird lists, and many birding software packages allow you to print out customized bird lists. Your child can even keep a bird list in a computer database, improving computer skills at the same time he or she learns about birds.

Encourage your child to write down notes about the bird's appearance and behavior, where the bird was seen and when, and what the weather conditions were like.

SAMPLE BIRD LIST

Morning bird walk, Cranberry Lake
April 12, 7:00 A.M.
Sunny, light breeze, about 70 degrees Fahrenheit
Walked around the lake and up the path into the woods. Watched a Gray Catbird taking a bath at the edge of the lake and saw a mockingbird chase off a crow. Then Red-tailed Hawk circled overhead, and a flock of crows took off to chase the hawk! A mother Mallard was swimming about with her seven babies. A male Red-winged Blackbird was singing on top of a cattail and flashing his red shoulders in the sun. Heard a Pileated Woodpecker drumming on a tree somewhere in the distance. A great morning!
Birds seen:
American Robin
Northern Mockingbird
Gray Catbird
Red-winged Blackbird
American Crow
Red-tailed Hawk
Mallard (with babies)
Pileated Woodpecker (heard only)

Eastern Bluebirds in the snow.

Chapter Four

BIRDWATCHING BASICS

So you have your binoculars, you're wearing good shoes and sunscreen, and you're carrying a guidebook. Where are all the birds?

Look

Birds are everywhere—just look around. Many species probably visit your backyard every day. Once your children start to notice birds, they'll begin to see them everywhere they go—from the gulls in the supermarket parking lot, to the pigeons living under the freeway bridges, to the honking geese migrating overhead in the fall. Your task is simply to point birds out and talk enthusiastically to your child about them. Your child's natural curiosity will do the rest.

Listen

But don't just look for birds—listen! Many birds will be found first by their songs and calls. Some night birds, like owls and Whip-poor-wills, are much easier to hear than to see. Plus, children have more acute hearing than do many adults. Once your children start listening for birds, you may be surprised by how often they find birds before you do.

Walk Quietly

Birds may fly away before you see them if you make too much noise. Successful birdwatching requires your child to move slowly and quietly. This may sound like a tall order to ask of a young child, but birdwatching carries great rewards in the form of interesting bird sightings. Only your child can decide if he or she is interested enough in finding birds to walk quietly.

On the other hand, very young children may be better off watching birds through a window. Perhaps you can take your child somewhere that the birds won't mind a running or laughing child too much. Try the zoo or a popular park to find ducks, pigeons, sparrows, and other birds that are used to people.

Birds are less likely to notice you if you stand next to a tree or behind a bush instead of out in the open. If your child is willing, try sitting quietly under a tree for a few minutes. Many birds will quickly learn to ignore you and will come surprisingly close.

Birdwatching should be a family affair, a memorable experience for old and young alike.

Go Early

The best time to see most birds is early in the morning, when they are first waking up. Birds are most active early in the day as they look for breakfast. Early morning is also when most birds sing. Try taking your child out to the woods or a meadow at dawn and enjoy the chorus as dozens of different birds greet the day.

Where to Find Birds

Start looking for birds in your own backyard. There are probably lots of birds living in and around your yard that your family has never even noticed. Try watching quietly through a window for a while, particularly with younger children who may run around and scare off birds before they get a chance to see them.

Different birds will use different parts of your yard. Encourage your child to look up high for birds flying overhead or bouncing around in the treetops. Closer to eye level, many birds will seek shelter inside bushes and shrubs. Other birds will be scratching around on the ground looking for seeds and insects. Some may take dirt baths

Birdbaths attract many birds, such as this Blue Jay.

to fluff their feathers. If you have water in your yard, birds will often come in for a drink or a splash. You can increase the number and variety of birds that visit your yard by adding birdfeeders, a birdbath, and birdhouses.

However, don't limit your child's backyard to the inside of your fence. Watching birds can introduce your child to a larger community as well. Here are some places to visit where birds can be found.

LOCAL PARKS

Particularly in urban areas, a park is like an oasis in the desert to birds. In fact, in desert areas, parks may be the only place for birds to find water easily, and they may therefore host a wide variety of bird visitors. They may also have the only large trees in the area.

EDGES

Places where one habitat meets another, such as where the woods meet a field, attract a wide variety of birds. Within a park, the areas where mown lawn meets bushes will offer more birds than the lawn alone. Water edges, like the bushes along a stream, will be particularly fruitful areas to search for birds.

WATER

Ponds, streams, and beaches all attract different kinds of birds. Try visiting different types of water and seeing what kinds of birds live in and near each one. Talk to your child about why different birds choose different homes.

WILDLIFE REFUGES

Refuges are areas set aside because they are particularly important to some kinds of animals or plants. Many refuges represent the only habitat of its kind in an area. A refuge may be, for example, the only marshland remaining in a sea of housing developments. If you live near a wildlife refuge, consider yourself lucky. Introducing your child to the different habitats and birds that live in the refuge should be a priority.

Window Strikes and Injured Birds

The windows of your house let you view your yard from the comfort of your home. Unfortunately, they can also prove to be a deadly temptation for birds. Sometimes birds won't realize that a window is a barrier, and they will fly into your windows and injure themselves. Windows may reflect the outside world and trick birds into thinking the glass is actually an extension of your yard. Sometimes birds may not see the windows at all and will fly into them thinking they can fly right through your house. In some cases, a bird may be fleeing a predator like a cat or a hawk and fly blindly into the window.

WHAT TO DO IF YOU FIND AN INJURED BIRD

If a bird strikes your window and survives, it may need a limited amount of your help. The major risk to the bird is being eaten by a neighborhood cat. To prevent this, pick up the bird with a towel and place it gently in a cardboard box or a large paper bag. Put the bird in a quiet, warm place.

If you have a wildlife refuge near you, visit it often. Development in an area often forces birds into refuges.

PREVENTING TRAGEDY

When a bird is injured or killed flying into your windows, it may be a very sad occasion for you and your child. Below are some ways to minimize the chances that a bird will hit your windows. These methods may also discourage territorial birds from fighting their reflections in your windows.

* Pull down your window shades or close your curtains during daylight hours.
* Break up the reflection on the outside of your windows with a window screen or netting.
* Install window awnings to block the sun from hitting the window and causing reflections.
* Attach bird silhouettes, removable decorative window "clings," or other things to your windows to provide a visible barrier.
* Move birdfeeders and baths well away from windows. Another option is to move them right up against windows (such as window feeders that attach directly to the glass) so that startled birds can't get up to "flight speed" before striking your windows.

Don't try to feed it or treat any visible injuries. If the bird is just stunned, it will quickly revive and you can release it where you found it. If it has injuries, call a wildlife rehabilitator. These people are licensed to help wild animals, but you are not. It is actually illegal for you to keep a wild bird, even an injured bird, in your home. Additionally, without proper training you are likely to do more harm than good if you try to treat the bird. Check your phone book or your state wildlife agency for the number of a rehabilitator near you.

"ORPHAN" BIRDS

If you find a baby bird that appears to be an orphan, your best bet is to leave it alone. Most "orphan" birds aren't orphaned at all. Even birds that have accidentally fallen out of a nest are usually still being cared for by their parents. If the bird has all its feathers, leave it where it is. The parents are probably nearby. If you have cats or dogs, keep them inside and away from the baby bird.

If you find a baby with few or no feathers and you can see the nest it came from, you can try to return it to its nest. Contrary to popular belief, the mother bird will not be frightened off by the smell of humans on her baby. If you can't return it to its nest, treat it like an injured bird—put it in a box and take it to a wildlife rehabilitator. Don't try to raise it yourself.

Keep Cats Indoors

One of the best ways to protect birds is to keep cats from catching them. Millions of small mammals and birds are killed by cats every year. Keep your cat indoors or only let it out during the middle of the day, when birds are least active. Never feed birds while your cat is outside. Putting a bell on your cat's collar may help warn birds in time to escape your cat, but this method is not foolproof.

Preschoolers can learn to use light-weight binoculars and become familiar with the more common birds in an area.

Chapter Five

Developing an Interest:
Toddlers and Preschoolers

At each stage of your child's life, there are different things you can do to encourage her interest in birds. It's never too early to start. From their earliest years, children are fascinated by the almost magical way that birds move through the air. Their bright colors and rapid movement can catch even an infant's attention.

Children who are just learning to walk and talk will notice birds and want to watch them, because these flying animals are unlike any other living creature in the child's world. Talk to your children about the birds they see. Teach them the names of different recognizable types of birds, like ducks and gulls. This will help your children learn that there are many kinds of birds and will increase their interest in learning about them.

Parents can also encourage their young children's interest by decorating their rooms with bird posters and mobiles. Wildlife posters, available from many wildlife organizations, will attract as much of your child's attention as pictures of television cartoon characters. As an added bonus, they will encourage your child to look out the window instead of watching television.

There are many wonderful children's books about birds that you can read to your child; later, your child can read them to herself. By choosing books that offer realistic depictions of birds and their lives, you can foster a genuine understanding of birds and the natural world.

Nature videotapes can be fun to watch with your child. Many environmental organizations offer learning tapes about birds that you can rent at your video store or check out of the library. Educational cable channels offer programming about wildlife around the world, including programs about birds that will catch your child's interest.

Placing a birdfeeder, birdhouse, or birdbath outside a child's window will let her see birds up close. Have your toddler help you fill the birdfeeder or bath. If your birdhouse attracts nesting birds, talk to your child about what sorts of food the mother (or father) bird is bringing to the babies.

A simple birdhouse outside a child's window will bring birds in close for easy viewing.

Take young children to the park or zoo to see a wider variety of birds. Large, unusual birds like parrots and flamingos will certainly be a topic of conversation. Talk to your child about the differences between these birds and the birds in your own backyard.

Feeding Wild Birds

Don't feed the ducks. As much fun as it might seem to take bread to the park to feed the ducks and geese, it is not a good idea for your child or the birds. Feeding wild animals like this (as opposed to offering natural foods in feeders) makes them dependent on food from humans and teaches them to associate food with humans. It also causes unnaturally large concentrations of birds to gather, which can foster disease epidemics that can wipe out whole populations.

Some birds, like geese and swans, can be very aggressive in seeking food or defending territory. These birds may injure your child in their pursuit of food. Never encourage your child to hold food out in her hand to a bird or any other wild animal.

Although it may seem like a contradiction to encourage the use of backyard birdfeeders and discourage other types of feeding, the two methods are very different. For one thing, commercial birdseed mixtures for backyard feeders are designed to offer healthy foods to birds. Stale bread is not a healthy food, and it fouls the water and ground if it is not eaten.

Feeders also bring birds in close to windows and may give a child a simple responsibility such as keeping the feeder filled.

Most wildlife organizations recommend offering only small amounts of birdseed in backyard feeders. This prevents the seed from rotting and reduces the numbers of birds that visit the feeders. Using feeders that only allow a few birds to visit at once will also reduce bird concentrations. These methods will help keep birds from passing diseases to each other and keep them from becoming dependent on you for all their food needs.

You can offer several different feeders with different types of food to increase the variety of birds that visit your yard without increasing the volume.

A gourmet seed mix will help you attract a wide variety of garden birds, from cardinals and finches to woodpeckers. Photo courtesy of Kaytee® Products, Inc.

Building Backyard Habitat

By making your backyard into better bird habitat, you can increase the number and type of birds that will visit you and your children. There are three components to a successful backyard bird habitat: food, water, and shelter. With very little effort, you can provide all three, making your yard a better place for birds and birdwatching.

FOOD

Birds don't necessarily need the food you provide, but they will happily eat it and let you and your child get a closer look at their behavior. During most of the year you don't need to worry about putting food out every day, because birds have plenty of other food sources to turn to. However, in the winter months birds may come to depend on the food you put out if more natural sources are covered with ice and snow, and you should put out a regular supply, particularly during heavy snowfalls or bitter cold.

Try providing several different kinds of food to attract a variety of birds. Seed mixtures, black oil sunflower seeds, thistle or nyjer seed, suet (rendered beef fat), sugar water, and fruit such as cut oranges or apples will all bring different birds to your yard. A salt block will also attract some birds. If you don't like the mess that seed hulls leave on your lawn, try offering pre-shelled seed mixtures.

Many choices in birdseeds, from basic mixes to specialty blends, as well as bells and cakes, are available. Choose what is right for your yard and the birds you wish to attract. Photo courtesy of Kaytee® Products, Inc.

Feeders often attract unusual and interesting birds, such as these Pine Siskins, and hold them for hours or days.

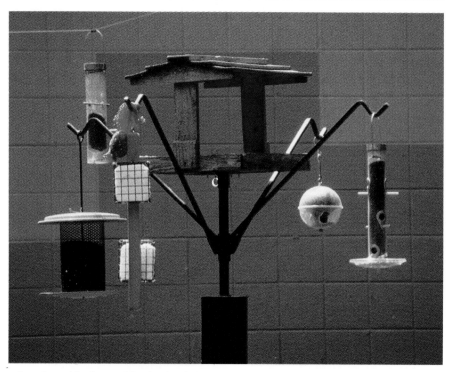

A variety of feeders and foods often helps draw a wider variety of birds.

It is healthier to offer seed from an elevated feeder than on the ground. Rotting food on the ground can spread diseases and attract unwanted rodents. If you hang feeders under an overhanging porch roof, they will stay dry and clean and seed hulls can be swept up easily. Make sure you place feeders away from shrubs that could conceal predators like hunting cats.

Some badly designed feeders can lure birds inside the seed dispenser when they are nearly empty; there trapped birds may panic and die. Make sure all feeder openings that a bird could access are smaller than an inch in diameter. Smaller feeders that hold less food will ensure that food doesn't stay in the feeder long enough to spoil.

WATER

Water is very important in the summer and winter months. Birds that won't come to feeders will gladly visit your backyard for a drink or a bath. A water source can be as simple as a pie pan full of water or as complex as a pond or stream. Dripping water is particularly attractive to birds; the sound will draw in birds from long distances. In the winter, in areas where the temperature drops below freezing at night, open water for drinking can become difficult for birds to find. If you offer water in winter, buy a heater made for underwater use (available at any wild-bird supply store) to keep the water from freezing.

Offer water in a shallow pool (no deeper than 3 inches) that can be easily cleaned and sterilized. Water that birds bathe in can become contaminated and then transmit diseases, so you should empty and clean your birdbath every week with hot, soapy water. Use a mild white vinegar solution to kill any algae that grow in the birdbath, but be sure to rinse the bath thoroughly before refilling it.

SHELTER

Birdhouses are only one way of providing shelter. You can also try landscaping part of your yard specifically for birds by planting dense shrubs or trees in which they can roost and nest. To help birds build nests, you and your child can put out nesting material in the spring. In a sheltered location visible from your windows, put out piles of string, yarn, small strips of cloth, and fur left over from brushing your cats or dogs. (String and yarn should be cut to short lengths to prevent entanglement.) Then sit back and watch the birds to see which materials they like best for constructing their nests.

If you are encouraging birds to come to your yard, you may want to stop using chemical insecticides or weedkillers, or at least use less of them. Birds that are exposed to pesticides can become ill or have trouble laying fertile eggs. Both the U. S. Department of Agriculture and the Environmental Protection Agency provide consumer information about alternatives to chemical pest control.

A ball of string and straw for nesting materials will attract birds during the spring and summer.

A male Anna's Hummingbird. Everyone notices hummingbirds, and they are easy to attract for close looks.

Chapter Six

EXPANDING HORIZONS:
SCHOOL-AGE CHILDREN
(AGES 6-12)

At this age children can begin to learn to identify birds based on subtler characteristics such as bill shape, habitat, or even sound (Chapter One includes tips on learning bird categories). Children can hear better than most adults and often will locate a bird by sound long before a parent notices that it's there. By this age most children are coordinated enough to begin to use binoculars successfully.

Teaching Tools

There are many things parents can do to encourage school-age children in their growing enjoyment of birds. A number of teaching tools can help your child learn more about birds and their behavior. Some methods may seem a little too much like school—but if your child is interested, learning about birds can become a game.

BIRD IDENTIFICATION GUIDES

School-age children will be ready to take a step up from simple picture books to bird guides that include more information about behavior and natural history. There are quite a few guides on the market that include the kind of odd and unusual facts about birds that will catch a youngster's interest. A new bird guide is a good gift for a long trip and can be enjoyed in a car or plane.

A parent should help a child become familiar with using any bird identification guide.

BIRD SONG RECORDINGS

Identifying birds by their voices—also known as "birding by ear"—can be a challenge. Even experienced birdwatchers can be stumped by an unfamiliar song. But listening to birds opens new opportunities for appreciating and understanding their lives. Birds use song to warn of dangers, to charm a mate, as well as to keep in touch with each other. By listening carefully to birds in the backyard, kids can begin to hear the different sounds that birds make under different situations.

Inside the home, kids can listen to recordings of bird songs that will help them learn which songs go with which birds. Many companies offer bird song recordings, and most libraries will let you check out these recordings. If you have a compact disc player, you may want to try to find bird recordings on CD that will let your kids go directly to the birds they are most interested in and easily replay songs to hear them again. Some tapes are organized to follow a particular bird guide, allowing kids to follow the pictures along with the songs.

Kids can also make their own recordings by putting a tape recorder next to a birdfeeder, birdbath, or nest box. The recording quality may not be great, but kids will have fun listening to baby birds begging for food or trying to figure out which birds visited their backyard.

BIRD VIDEOTAPES

Several companies make excellent videotapes to help in bird identification. When it's too cold or rainy to watch birds outside, these tapes serve as a great substitute. Some tapes focus on particular groups of birds; others are more general. Some offer tips on birding by ear or on building birdhouses or other projects.

Rainy Day Projects

There are plenty of projects for you and your child to do together for fun, even on rainy days.

FLASH CARDS

Flash cards with pictures or photographs of a bird on the front and the bird's name and some natural history information on the back are commercially available from many sources, but you and your child may want to make your own instead.

Some birds sing songs that are easy to learn and remember. The Carolina Wren may have one of the loudest songs of any common small bird.

To make flash cards, cut out pictures of birds from old magazines, calendars, and other sources. Many children's magazines print nice pictures of common birds. Be sure to keep information from photo captions or articles that includes the name of the bird. Paste the pictures on the front of each card and write the names of the birds on the back. Then look up information about the birds in a bird guide and add it to the card. Children may learn information better if they look it up and write it down themselves. The process of making these flash cards is sure to leave an indelible impression in their memories.

When your child is done with the cards, you can donate them to a children's hospital, a bird club, or a school, where other children can use them to learn about birds.

BIRD SILHOUETTES

Many types of birds are recognizable just by their body shape or the way they perch in a tree. In fact, some bird guides include silhouettes in the margins as a quick reference for looking up birds. Learning basic shape categories will help your child quickly identify a new bird as a type of duck or hawk or woodpecker, for example. Some manufacturers offer stencils for bird silhouettes— or you can make your own.

45

To make silhouettes, find representative pictures of birds in a bird guide. In other words, find the picture of a duck that most looks like a duck, the owl that most looks like an owl, and so on. Using tracing paper, carefully draw just the outline of the bird. Enlarge the drawing on a photocopier. Use the large picture as a pattern to cut out a silhouette of each bird from black construction paper or cardboard.

Silhouettes can be used in different forms. Kids can make them into flash cards like those described above. They can decorate your windows, which will also help real birds avoid flying into the glass, or you can make them into a mobile to decorate a child's room. The silhouettes will remind your child of the different bird categories and make them a familiar part of your child's world.

As a child gets older, there is a natural interest in expanding the birding area well beyond the backyard.

Leaving the Nest

A child's backyard need not end at the fence or at the end of the lawn. School-age children will also enjoy longer outings and hands-on projects that will expand their world. Birdwatching can become a path to a larger appreciation of the environment around a child.

Nature hikes are a fun way to watch birds, enjoy some family time, and learn about the environment. Many parks, zoos, museums, and wildlife refuges have self-guided nature walks that offer information about the plants and animals you are likely to see along the way. Most refuges also have visitor centers that offer educational programs and information about the plants and animals that live there.

You may also choose your own path and find a hiking trail that offers a varying landscape with different habitats for different birds. Any of these walks will let your kids see a larger variety of birds than may be visible from your yard.

As you walk, talk to your family about what they are seeing. Notice the changing vegetation as you move up a hill or toward a stream. Different kinds of trees and other plants grow near water or on the sheltered slope of a hill. Do different birds frequent these areas as well?

At night, try listening for night birds. Whether you're out camping or just pulling the car over next to a park, you may hear many different kinds of night birds, from owls to Whip-poor-wills. Many refuges and bird clubs offer moonlit walks with guides that can help your kids learn to recognize the unique sounds of different night birds.

During annual events like International Migratory Bird Day, held each year on the second Saturday in May, many refuges, parks, zoos, and museums will hold special events with activities and programs about birds. Kids will particularly enjoy the live bird demonstrations at many of these events. See the Resources chapter for a list of annual events that you can put on your calendar.

Pick vacation destinations that offer opportunities to see bird species not found locally. If you live in the Midwest, think about a trip to the desert. If you live near sea level, try a trip to the mountains. Boat trips will provide looks at pelagic birds, which spend most of their lives at sea.

Encourage children to look for birds wherever they are. Watching for birds from a car window can liven up a long trip.

Live Bird Demonstrations

Local nature centers and zoos periodically offer demonstrations of bird banding that your family may enjoy. Bird banding is a research tool that involves capturing wild birds and placing a plastic or metal identification ring around their leg. The identification number on each ring is recorded with the U.S. Fish and Wildlife Service by licensed bird banders. When banded birds are recaptured in the future, biologists can look up the information about the original banding and learn about the bird's age and the distance it has traveled.

Banding is an invaluable technique for biologists to gather more information about the lives of wild birds. Banding demonstrations let your kids see birds up close, find out about the science behind studies of birds, and maybe even handle a bird themselves.

Rehabilitation centers at zoos or wildlife agencies offer close looks at wild birds that have been injured and are unable to survive in the wild. These birds are comfortable around humans and are often used in educational programs. These centers teach kids about the threats that wild birds face, like fast-moving cars and power lines. They will also help your children appreciate the difficulty of caring for a wild bird.

Learning about bird banding will increase a teenager's knowledge of birds and also help develop an interest in birds in general.

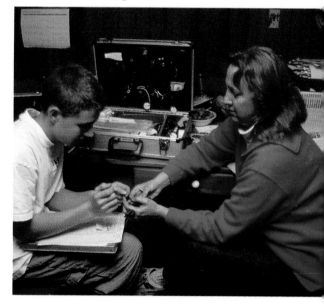

Projects

Kids love to get their hands dirty in the backyard. By helping to improve the bird habitat around your home, your kids can get dirty, have fun, and make a difference in

LOOKING FOR LEFTOVERS

Birds leave clues behind that will help you figure out who has been visiting your backyard. With your child, you can look for seed hulls, dropped feathers, footprints, and other evidence of bird activity.

Check for crushed or broken seeds or nuts. If they don't have teethmarks on them, chances are they were eaten by a bird.

Broken eggshells may mean a bird has a nest nearby—but not necessarily. Many mother birds carry eggshells far from the nest after their babies hatch. If you find a nest, watch carefully to see if any birds are using it. If it isn't being used, look at it closely. Can you tell what kinds of materials the birds used to make the nest? Sometimes birds will use manmade objects like string in their nests, as well as sticks and grass. Some nests are so distinctive they can tell you what kind of bird made them. Your child may enjoy checking out a book from the library with pictures of different kinds of bird nests.

Footprints won't tell you exactly what species of birds visited your yard, but they can tell you what kinds of birds came by. Webbed feet mean water birds. Birds with three toes pointing forward and one pointing back are perching birds. Woodpeckers have X-shaped feet—two toes pointing forward, two pointing backward.

Out in the woods, you may be able to find owl pellets. Owls swallow their prey whole, then regurgitate the parts they cannot digest, like bones, fur, and feathers. These parts make a compact pellet that you can tease apart to see what the owl ate.

Examine the feathers you find—can you tell what part of the bird they came from? Are they fluffy down or long wing or tail feathers? Are there any clues to what kind of bird they came from?

Don't keep any feathers or eggshells. A federal law called the Migratory Bird Treaty Act makes it illegal to keep eggs, nests, or feathers from most birds, even after the birds are done with them. Instead of collecting these items, you can draw pictures or take photographs of them. Taking photographs is also a great way to preserve "evidence" of bird visits like footprints.

the number and variety of birds that will visit.

A bird's habitat must include food, water, and shelter. Your family can help add all three to your yard, then enjoy watching as birds flock in.

By offering a wider variety of foods, you will attract a wider variety of birds (up to a point, of course). There are many commercial birdfeeders available that your child can help hang and keep filled, or you and your child can make some simple and inexpensive feeders.

If your yard doesn't have a natural water source, like a pond or stream, adding water will bring new birds in droves. A birdbath can be as simple as a pie pan or Frisbee™ filled with water. Birds like fresh water as much as you, so put your kids in charge of keeping the birdbath filled and clean.

Any child can help put in colorful flowers to attract birds and their insect prey.

Decorating around a dish-style birdbath can be an interesting project for kids. Kids can dig a wide, shallow hole to put the dish in so that the edges are flush with ground level. Small rocks and sticks placed around the edge of the pool will encourage birds to linger next to the pool to sun themselves after their drink or bath. A strong forked twig stuck in the ground offers a perch from which birds can look for danger before entering the bath.

Planting new bushes or flowers that offer food and shelter involves many hours of fun digging in the dirt. Check with your local plant nursery for advice on bird-friendly native plants and the best time for planting. Your kids can keep the new plants watered and watch them for new visitors.

Another interesting addition to your yard is a dust bath. Many birds "bathe" in loose dirt, perhaps to remove oil and debris from their feathers. Your child will be happy to make a dirt pile in your garden that doesn't get him in trouble. Choose an out of the way area for the dust bath. Fill it with loose, dry soil, then keep an eye out for the miniature tornadoes that birds stir up when they toss the dirt over their backs.

PLASTER CASTS OF FOOTPRINTS

Making plaster casts of bird tracks is a good way of preserving them for further study. You can buy quick-setting plaster of Paris at any hardware or hobby shop. Make a corral with a 2- to 3-inch-high strip of cardboard bent in a circle. The circle should be wide enough to enclose large bird footprints.

Mix the plaster with water in an old jar or can until it reaches a runny consistency. Place the corral around the tracks and fill it up about halfway. Leave the plaster alone until it is hard set. Remove the collar and carefully lift up the cast. Wash any clinging dirt off the cast with cold water.

Easy Feeders that Children Can Make (With a Little Help from Mom and Dad)

There are lots of easy birdfeeders that school-age children can make themselves. Here are a few to try:

Pine Cone Peanut Butter Feeder

Materials:
- Pinecone
- Strong string
- Peanut butter (smooth or chunky)
- Birdseed (any kind will do)

Tie the string to the wide end of a pinecone. Using a spoon, fill the cracks and crevices of the pinecone with peanut butter, then roll it in birdseed. Hang the feeder where you can see it from the window, then sit back and watch.

Expected visitors: Woodpeckers, chickadees, nuthatches, titmice.

Net Bag Suet Feeder

Materials:
- Plastic net bag, like the ones some fruit and vegetables are sold in
- Strong string
- Suet (beef fat)*
- Birdseed (any kind will do)
- Optional: raisins, nutmeats

Melt the suet in a double boiler (mom or dad should help with this). After it cools, mold it into a ball and roll it in birdseed. (If you are adding raisins or nuts, mix them into the suet before rolling it in birdseed.) Drop it into the net bag. Tie the bag tightly closed with string, leaving plenty of string to hang up your suet feeder outside.

Expected visitors: Woodpeckers, chickadees, nuthatches, titmice.

A suet feeder is easily made from an old onion bag and works as well as a purchased feeder.

Caution: This feeder doesn't work well in hot weather, as the suet can spoil or melt and stick to the bird's feathers. But many winter visitors will love this feeder.

*Ask at the supermarket meat counter for beef fat. Be sure to ask for short suet, or kidney suet, instead of stringy suet. Make sure that it is white, firm, and fresh. Butchers may even give it to you for free if you tell them it's for the birds.

FRUIT FEEDER
Materials:
• Nails
• Oranges, apples, bananas

Hammer a nail with a small head into a tree or post at a height where the child can reach it easily. Leave about 2 inches of the nail sticking out. Cut apples or oranges in half, bananas in sections with the peel still on. Impale half an apple or orange or a section of banana onto the nail.

Oranges attract orioles and tanagers and are easily placed on simple feeders.

Expected visitors: Orioles, tanagers, thrushes, some woodpeckers, hummingbirds.

MILK CARTON SEED FEEDER
Materials:
• Empty milk carton (half gallon, quart, or pint)
• Wooden dowels (1/4-inch diameter) cut about 6 inches long
• Strong string
• Mixed birdseed or black oil sunflower seeds

Clean the milk carton carefully with hot water and soap. Rinse thoroughly. Cut 1-inch square (or round) holes in all four sides of the carton. Two holes—on opposite sides of the carton—should be slightly higher than the other two. With a nail or a skewer, punch small holes in the carton about an inch below the bottom of each hole. Push dowels through the holes so that they go all the way through and out the opposite side. Fill the carton with birdseed or sunflower seeds. Put the top of the carton back together the way it was before it was opened, and punch holes at both ends of the peak. String thread through the holes in the carton so that it holds the top closed. Hang your feeder.

Expected visitors: Almost everyone! Particularly sparrows, finches, chickadees, titmice, cardinals.

Birdwatching—or birding—is a hobby for all ages and life styles.

Chapter Seven

A LIFELONG HABIT:
ADOLESCENTS
(AGES 13 AND UP)

As children enter their teens, some may lose interest in the outdoors and in birds. Birding, however, can offer adolescents a sense of purpose, whether it be the simple goal of seeing a new bird, the pride of building and maintaining backyard bird habitat, or the accomplishment of helping local groups with conservation projects.

Teens can become more involved by taking birding, ornithology, or field ecology classes at local museums, nature centers, or community colleges. These types of classes are aimed at many different levels of experience, so your teen will be able to find one that fits. This is an excellent way for teens to learn about how birds are related to each other and their environment.

Teens will also meet other birdwatchers in these classes and find new people to go birdwatching with.

There are a number of opportunities for teens to volunteer and help add to the body of knowledge about birds. During spring and fall migrations, scientists and bird enthusiasts team up to count birds to learn more about their populations, migrations routes, ranges, and habitats. Teens of any level of expertise will be welcome assistants on bird censuses. One big census, the Audubon Christmas Bird Count, happens every year in December and early January.

Some censuses involve capturing and banding birds. With a little training, your teen may be able to help remove birds from the special nets used in these projects and take the special measurements that help determine a bird's age, sex, and health. All official bird banders must be licensed by the U.S. Fish and Wildlife Service, and laws regarding their assistants vary from state to state. Even if your teen is not allowed to handle the birds, he or she can still help with recording data. At the same time, your teen will be gaining knowledge about birds.

In the fall (and, in some areas, the spring), birdwatchers conduct hawk watches to observe migrating raptors. A raptor is a member of the group of predatory or meat-eating birds that includes hawks, eagles, falcons, ospreys, and vultures. Hawkwatchers, as they are popularly called, count the raptors as they pass overhead. They also record information about the birds' ages and the weather conditions. Your teens can help out by

Visiting a hawk watch is a great opportunity to meet other birders and see incredible displays of hawks, eagles, and other birds of prey.

spotting hawks and recording data. Talk to your local bird club about the best places in your area to watch the hawk migration.

Bird rehabilitation centers often need volunteers to help feed injured birds and clean cages. Teens may be able to assist rehabilitators in their educational efforts when they take their "working birds" on outings to schools and other groups.

Amateur bird groups usually have educational and community projects of their own. Through these groups, your teen can help put up birdfeeders or houses at nursing homes, hospitals, nature centers, and wildlife refuges. By helping with bird talks and slide shows for scout and school groups, your teen can gain confidence in public speaking and enjoy passing on knowledge and love of birds to younger children.

Birdhouses are easy to build and maintain and often start children on a long-term interest in birdwatching.

Backyard Birdhouses

Teens can construct a simple birdhouse with a minimum of tools. All you really need is four walls, a roof and a floor, a way for birds to get in, and a way to hang the birdhouse. Nearly all cavity-nesting birds—birds that nest in natural holes in trees—will use an enclosed birdhouse. Birds prefer simple, cozy structures in natural wood colors rather than painted ornamental structures.

One aspect of a birdhouse most determines which kind of bird will move in—the size of the entrance hole. Two species of birds that are not native to North America will quickly take over most birdhouses in many settings: House Sparrows and European Starlings. These birds, introduced to this country by European settlers nostalgic for birds from home, have driven many native North American species to the brink of extinction by competing with them for nest sites.

By building a birdhouse that only lets in the birds you want, your teen can help native birds. House Sparrows and European Starlings cannot get into birdhouses with entrance holes smaller than $1\,^1/_2$ inches in diameter. Nearly any birdhouse with a smaller entrance hole will quickly be occupied by a wren, nuthatch, chickadee, titmouse, or other cavity-nesting bird.

The other important aspects of any birdhouse are the roof, a means of access for cleaning, and placement in your yard. All birdhouses should have slanted roofs that hang over the entrance to keep out rain and snow. Where possible, they should be placed on the northern, cooler side of a tree or house. All birdhouses need to have a hinged side so they can be opened for easy cleaning after the young birds have left the nest.

For more information on the dimensions of birdhouses, check out the U.S. Fish and Wildlife Service's "pamphlets" online (See Resources). Their site also has information about birdfeeders, landscaping for birds, and migratory songbird conservation.

Bird Behavior

Once your teen has learned to identify all the birds in your neighborhood, what's left to look at? Plenty. Every bird is different—just because you've seen one robin doesn't mean the next one can't be interesting. Here are a few things for your teen to think about the next time he or she looks at a bird.

A peanut butter feeder may attract odd birds and allow a study of their pecking order.

FEEDING

What are birds eating? When they have a variety of foods to choose from, which ones do they seem to prefer? Teens can try to answer these questions in your own backyard by using a food testing tray. A testing tray is a flat tray with divided compartments (a screened bottom will prevent rainwater from collecting and spoiling the seed). By putting a measured amount of a different food in each compartment, your teen can see which foods the local birds like best by watching which seeds disappear first. By watching birds feed, your teen can see which birds prefer which foods.

INTERACTIONS

All birds have a "pecking order," both within and between species. Some birds always seem to get the first choice of food and the best nest sites. Sometimes this depends on the age or the size of the individual bird; sometimes it just depends on which species is the most aggressive. Your teen can watch birds at your backyard feeder to see which birds will chase others away and which birds feed happily side by side. Some interactions have to do with actual threats from other birds. Many birds will mob Blue Jays and crows, which often steal other birds' eggs. Crows, in turn, will mob hawks and owls, which may eat other birds.

An American Robin's nest and eggs often are easy to see and sure to draw interest.

Courtship and Nesting

The interactions between mated birds are some of the most interesting. Many male birds court females in the spring by bringing them "gifts" of food or nesting material or by performing complicated dances or beautiful songs. Once a pair has mated and settled in your yard, your teen can watch to see which aspects of nesting involve both birds and which involve only one. In some species only the male bird does the nest-building, sitting on eggs, and bringing food to hatchlings. In other species both male and female birds cooperate in these tasks.

After the baby birds have fledged—grown their adult flight feathers—they can look almost indistinguishable from their parents. However, most young birds will continue to beg for food from their parents for days or weeks after they have left the nest. Your teen can learn the differences between the look of young birds and older birds by watching to see which birds exhibit classic begging behavior—wings stretched and fluttering, head bowed low, mouth open.

Age

In many bird species there are distinct plumage changes between a bird's early and later years. In gulls and eagles, for example, it is possible to tell the age of a bird up to the third or fourth year of life. By learning these subtle plumage differences, your teen can stop looking at a gull as "just another Herring Gull," and start classifying the birds as "Herring Gull, second summer," for example. A bird book that specializes in these distinctions makes a great gift for a teenage birdwatcher.

It is never acceptable to disturb nesting birds. This White-crowned Sparrow is feeding its brood.

Chapter Eight

BIRDWATCHING ETHICS

Learning to enjoy birds also involves learning to respect them. Watching birds without disturbing them is an art that is best learned young. The first time you take your children birdwatching, set a good example by moving quietly and staying far enough away not to scare the birds.

No matter how much your child wants to see a particular bird, it is never acceptable to do the following:

- Scare parent birds off the nest or repeatedly peek into bird nests to see the babies
- Trespass on private property
- Disturb sensitive habitat that may be crushed or destroyed if you walk through it.

Even though your child might enjoy collecting feathers, eggshells, or birds' nests, don't allow it. The Migratory Bird Treaty Act is a federal law that makes it illegal to collect feathers, nests, or eggshells—even after the bird is done using them. While this law is rarely enforced on private citizens who just collect a couple of feathers, it's simply not a good idea.

BIRDING ETHICS

The American Birding Association, one of the oldest birdwatching organizations in the United States, has developed a code of birding ethics that you may find useful in guiding your child's birdwatching experiences.

Everyone who enjoys birds and birding must always respect wildlife, its environment, and the rights of others. In any conflict of interest between birds and birders, the welfare of the birds and their environment comes first.

CODE OF BIRDING ETHICS

1. Promote the welfare of birds and their environment.
   (a) Support the protection of important bird habitat.
   (b) To avoid stressing birds or exposing them to danger, exercise restraint and caution during observation, photography, sound recording, or filming.
   Limit the use of recordings and other methods of attracting birds, and never use such methods in heavily birded areas or for attracting any species that is Threatened, Endangered, or of Special Concern, or is rare in your local area.
   Keep well back from nests and nesting colonies, roosts, display areas, and important feeding sites. In such sensitive areas, if there is a need for extended observation, photography, filming, or recording, try to use a blind or hide and take advantage of natural cover.
   Use artificial light sparingly for filming or photography, especially for close-ups.
   (c) Before advertising the presence of a rare bird, evaluate the potential for disturbance to the bird, its surroundings, and other people in the area, and proceed only if access can be controlled, disturbance minimized, and permission has been obtained from private landowners. The sites of rare nesting birds should be divulged only to the proper conservation authorities.
   (d) Stay on roads, trails, and paths where they exist; otherwise keep habitat disturbance to a minimum.
2. Respect the law and the rights of others.
   (a) Do not enter private property without the owner's explicit permission.
   (b) Follow all laws, rules, and regulations governing use of roads and public areas, both at home and abroad.

(c) Practice common courtesy in contacts with other people. Your exemplary behavior will generate goodwill with birders and non-birders alike.

3. Ensure that feeders, nest structures, and other artificial bird environments are safe.

a) Keep dispensers, water, and food clean and free of decay or disease. It is important to feed birds continually during harsh weather.

(b) Maintain and clean nest structures regularly.

(c) If you are attracting birds to an area, ensure the birds are not exposed to predation from cats and other domestic animals, or dangers posed by artificial hazards.

4. Group birding, whether organized or impromptu, requires special care. Each individual in the group, in addition to the obligations spelled out in Items #1 and #2, has responsibilities as a Group Member.

(a) Respect the interests, rights, and skills of fellow birders, as well as people participating in other legitimate outdoor activities. Freely share your knowledge and experience, except where code 1(c) applies. Be especially helpful to beginning birders.

(b) If you witness unethical birding behavior, assess the situation, and intervene if you think it prudent. When interceding, inform the person(s) of the inappropriate action and attempt, within reason, to have it stopped. If the behavior continues, document it and notify appropriate individuals or organizations.

Group Leader Responsibilities [amateur and professional trips and tours].

(c) Be an exemplary ethical role model for the group. Teach through word and example.

(d) Keep groups to a size that limits impact on the environment and does not interfere with others using the same area.

Ensure birds are not exposed to predation from cats and other domestic animals at feeders, birdhouses, and birdbaths.

(e) Ensure everyone in the group knows of and practices this code.

(f) Learn and inform the group of any special circumstances applicable to the areas being visited (e.g., no tape recorders allowed).

(g) Acknowledge that professional tour companies bear a special responsibility to place the welfare of birds and the benefits of public knowledge ahead of the company's commercial interests. Ideally, leaders should keep track of tour sightings, document unusual occurrences, and submit records to appropriate organizations.

Please follow this code and distribute and teach it to others.

RESOURCES

Bird Activities and Events

Several web sites include detailed calendars listing bird-related events. One of the best sites is the American Birding Association's calendar at http://www.americanbirding.org/evntgen.htm. This site lists events and birding festivals, sorted by date and by location.

EARTH DAY

Every year on April 22, America celebrates Earth Day. Because Earth Day falls in the middle of spring bird migration in many parts of the country, bird clubs and other environmental organizations often focus events on birds. Check with your local bird club for birding events or try your local newspaper for a list of local Earth Day activities.

INTERNATIONAL MIGRATORY BIRD DAY

Held each year on the second Saturday in May, this event is celebrated with birding festivals around the country. Many local bird clubs will hold special events like bird-banding demonstrations and live bird shows to highlight the wonders of the annual spring bird migration.

NATIONAL AUDUBON SOCIETY BIRDATHONS

Each spring, usually in April and May, Audubon bird club chapters hold contests between teams of birdwatchers to see who can find the most bird species within a single day of birding. Many teams do this just for fun and to help raise money for the conservation programs of their local chapter and the National Audubon Society.

NATIONAL AUDUBON SOCIETY CHRISTMAS BIRD COUNT

Christmas Bird Counts, held throughout the months of December and January, are great ways for kids to get involved in their local bird clubs. Since Christmas Day 1900, the counts have provided valuable information on the types and numbers of birds that live in particular areas during the early winter months. Both experienced and beginning birders can participate in the all-day censuses.

Birding and Nature Organizations

AMERICAN BIRDING ASSOCIATION

The American Birding Association is one of the oldest clubs for birdwatchers in North America. It's good for beginners as well as more advanced birdwatchers, as it offers information on bird identification, conservation, and education. The club allows birdwatchers to network with others across the country. The club produces a magazine, *Birding*, and a newsletter, *Winging It*, that offer monthly information on various bird topics.
P.O. Box 6599
Colorado Springs, CO 80934
phone: 719-578-1614
e-mail: member@aba.org
website: www.americanbirding.org

CORNELL LAB OF ORNITHOLOGY

The Cornell Lab of Ornithology is a membership institute dedicated to the study, appreciation, and conservation of birds. The Lab aims to foster understanding about nature and to contribute to efforts to protect biological diversity through research, education, and citizen-science programs.
Membership Department
P.O. Box 11
Ithaca, NY 14851
phone: 607-254-2425
website: www.ornith.cornell.edu/

INSTITUTE FOR BIRD POPULATIONS— BIRD BANDING CLASSES

Designed to provide both amateur birders and professional biologists with the skills necessary to participate in monitoring and research programs involving bird banding.
P.O. Box 1346
Point Reyes Station, CA 94956-1346
phone: 415-663-1436
e-mail: dfroehlich@birdpop.org
website: http://www.birdpop.org

NATIONAL AUDUBON SOCIETY

Founded in 1905, its mission is to conserve and restore natural ecosystems, focusing on birds and other wildlife, for the benefit of humanity and the earth's biological diversity. Publishes *Audubon* magazine.

700 Broadway
New York, NY 10003
phone: 212-979-3000
e-mail for membership information:
join@audubon.org
website: www.audubon.org

NATIONAL BIRDFEEDING SOCIETY

A non-profit group dedicated to making birdfeeding better for people and the birds. Through education and research, the Society helps its members improve the environment outside their own back doors.
P.O. Box 23L
Northbrook, IL 60065-0023.
phone: 847-272-0135
e-mail: Feedbirds@aol.com
website: www.birdfeeding.org/

STUDENT CONSERVATION ASSOCIATION

Offers volunteer opportunities and expense-paid internships in resource management, including some related to birds. Website contains a searchable listing of such opportunities.
SCA Membership
World Wide Web Desk
689 River Road
P.O. Box 550
Charleston, NH 03603
phone: 603-543-1700
website: www.sca-inc.org

U.S. FISH AND WILDLIFE SERVICE

Includes information on backyard birding, national wildlife refuges, bird conservation, and lists of threatened and endangered species.
website: www.fws.gov

YOUTH BIRDER WEB RING

A website with links to resources for teenage birdwatchers worldwide. Also includes information on how to join online chat rooms devoted to birdwatching.
website: http://udel.edu/~france/teenbirding.html

RARE BIRD ALERTS

Many states and cities have special hotlines for reporting and learning about sightings of rare or unusual birds. Looking for a rare bird, particularly with other birdwatchers, can be a fun way to see new birds, meet new people, and visit new areas. The American Birding Association has a list of Rare Bird Alert phone numbers nationwide on its website at: http://www.americanbirding.org/wgrbaadd.htm

MORE INFORMATION ON FEEDERS, BIRDHOUSES, ETC.

The Baltimore Bird Club has a great website with information on all aspects of backyard birding, including feeders, houses, landscaping, and backyard bird problems.
website: http://www.bcpl.lib.md.us/%7Etross/by/backyard.html

Additional Reading

The Birder's Handbook by Ehrlich, Dobkin, and Wheye, 1988. Simon and Schuster, New York.

The Complete Birder: A Guide to Better Birding by Jack Connor, 1988. Houghton Mifflin Co., Boston.

The Expert's Guide to Backyard Birdfeeding by Bill Adler and Heidi Hughes, 1990. Crown Publishers, New York.

Backyard Bird Feeding, 1988. U.S. Fish & Wildlife Service, Washington, DC 20240.

Homes for Birds, 1990. U.S. Fish & Wildlife Service, Washington, DC 20240.

Favorite Birds: Laser Cut Plastic Stencils, by Ruth Soffer. Dover Publishers.

Field Guides

Birds of North America: A Guide to Field Identification, Revised Edition, 1983. Zim, Herbert S., Robbins, Chandler S., Bruun, Bertel, Singer, Arthur, Eds. Golden Press, New York.

Field Guide to the Birds of North America, Third Edition, 1999. Bloom, Erik and Dunn, John L., Eds. National Geographic Society, Washington, DC.

The Audubon Society Field Guide to North American Birds, Eastern Region or Western Region, 1994. Bull, John and Farrand, Jr., John, Eds. Alfred A. Knopf, New York.

Advanced Birding, by Kenn Kaufman, 1990. Houghton Mifflin Co., New York.

Stokes Field Guide to Birds, Eastern Region or Western Region, by Donald and Lillian Stokes, 1996. Little, Brown and Co., New York.

Hawks, by William S. Clark and Brian K. Wheeler, 1987. Houghton Mifflin Co., New York.

Warblers, by Jon Dunn and Kimball Garrett, 1997. Houghton Mifflin Co., New York.

INDEX

Page numbers in **bold** indicate photos